MW00563354

mother

mother

m.s. RedCherries

penguin books

PENGUIN BOOKS
An imprint of Penguin Random House LLC
penguinrandomhouse.com

Copyright © 2024 by m.s. RedCherries
Penguin Random House supports copyright. Copyright fuels creativity, encourages diverse voices,
promotes free speech, and creates a vibrant culture. Thank you for buying an authorized edition of
this book and for complying with copyright laws by not reproducing, scanning, or distributing
any part of it in any form without permission. You are supporting writers and allowing
Penguin Random House to continue to publish books for every reader.

Excerpts from "Thirteen Ways of Looking at an Indian" by Anita Endrezze.
Used by permission of the author.

Pages 125–127 constitute an extension of this copyright page.

LIBRARY OF CONGRESS CATALOGING-IN-PUBLICATION DATA
Names: RedCherries, M. S., author.
Title: Mother / m.s. RedCherries.
Description: [New York] : Penguin Books, an imprint of Penguin Random House
LLC, 2024. | Series: Penguin poets |
Identifiers: LCCN 2024004160 (print) | LCCN 2024004161 (ebook) |
ISBN 9780143137832 (paperback) | ISBN 9780593511947 (ebook)
Subjects: LCGFT: Poetry.
Classification: LCC PS3618.E4264 M68 2024 (print) |
LCC PS3618.E4264 (ebook) |
DDC 811/.6—dc23/eng/20240202
LC record available at https://lccn.loc.gov/2024004160
LC ebook record available at https://lccn.loc.gov/2024004161

Printed in the United States of America
1st Printing

Set in Adobe Caslon Pro
Designed by Catherine Leonardo

to my mothers,

Very early in my life it was too late.

—Marguerite Duras

Naa hetsėstseha naeveno'nòhtse'anonėstse nemenestotòtse
tsetao'seve'šeo'omėhoxovestavatse

And now we are looking for songs that will
help us as we travel on

Ve'kesòhnestoohe
Dr. Richard Littlebear

Contents

Author's Note / xv

I

america / 3

[redacted] / 5

to [fall] and give / 6

you make me big / 7

we let no grief / 8

farther hellos / 9

keeping stillness / 10

talking back to me / 11

the end cannot be me / 13

engine injun / 14

america never looked for us / 23

listening to stay / 24

driving around looking for you / 25

only as old as we've been told / 26

/ mythos / 28

will we return? / 31

i don't have dream words / 33

the sky below you / 34

spinning air / 35

running roads above and away / 37

city thirst / 39

when quiet tangle speaks / 41

i lost all the nights / 42

rearview / 45

all air going north and a walk outside / 46

seeing by night / 48

measure of life through light / 49

the dream is dreamt / 50

you are the arc holding necessity / 52

make a new millennia / 54

under an illuminated same / 55

[somewhere] and kept / 59

i watch you but you do not watch me / 60

this is what kafka really meant when he wished to be a red indian / 63

the blood on your shirt is mine / 64

hover our grey / 66

hustle the roads / 67

driveway dreams / 68

eyes wide and a drive so fast / 71

shadow your best / 72

the headlights shine toward you / 75

II

hover their grey / 79

closing my eyes to see straight / 80

tour of the hemispheres / 81

melting in whisper / 82

red is the only color i see / 83

finding tomorrow / 84

running into and away / 85

there under an illuminated same / 86

october song / 87

mother, / 88

hymn eden / 90

how we're here / 91

you heard me first in the end / 92

red tilts home / 93

seeing the end / 95

in the quietest way / 96

will you look for me at all / 101

how must we be / 102

riding the highway 212 / 103

new mass / 105

searching the middle for you / 109

we slept at last / 112

july 1969 / 114

thisiswhere / 117

exodus / 119

Acknowledgments / 125

A Note about "red tilts home" / 127

Author's Note

mother is entirely a work of fiction. The names, characters, and incidents portrayed in it are the work of the author's imagination. Any resemblance to real persons, living or otherwise, is purely coincidental.

I

america

country eat country
an apocalypse in miniature

[redacted]

And when the woman ran from her house to the front of the BIA
building, and was told that she could not see her daughter because her
daughter was on her way to a residential school with the Dakotas and that
she would stay there because she was going to learn and stay with the
people who took her from the woman's house and onto a bus waiting at the
front of the BIA building, and when the woman tried to know where her
daughter was, she was taken and put on a bus to a hospital in the dakotas
because she was told she had too much sadness and that she would be
healed from the sadness which had taken her from her house to the front
of the BIA building and onto a waiting bus that would take her from the
mountains into the flat plains onto a gravel road up to a big brick building
with an american flag in front, where she would stay until her sadness went
away and when it didn't go away, her daughter, forty years later, seeking to
find her in her own sadness, found the woman's hospital records which
showed the woman being diagnosed with 'delusional melancholia,' and
when the woman died in her bed at twenty-six, she was laid alongside
another one hundred and twenty patients, all of whom now lay buried
between the 4th and 5th fairway of the Hiawatha Golf Club in canton,
south dakota.

to [fall] and give

My mother was born into a place crumbled between worlds. She stepped off an autumn ladder and down into the grass below, where she lay beside her family.

Living in a wooden house, deep in the hills of montana, she grew up during a bad, but not the worst time. A bad and confusing time. White people wanted to be Indians and Indians wanted to be left alone. The American Indian Movement was forming, and all Indians sought return, in some way or another, to their traditional ways. Many served in Vietnam, like my uncle. "Proud and brave" what the americans like to call Indians, true, nevertheless.

My mother was the proudest and bravest Indian I knew, standing so tall the clouds looked at her from both sides.

Born in an unkind century, my mother was remarkably Indian. She had black hair, darkskin and could speak our language. She lived generations in an open burial that illuminated generations.

She is a micro-blip of chasm that erodes the universe. She said that we try to bury our histories and find our futures, the ones we want to forget but always remember.

She pointed to a hawk in the sky, but it turned out to be a plastic bag. She was always a slippery marble-edged memory on its face.

But when she spoke, I listened.

you make me big

When I was born, I was relieved—a collected calm washed over me, as part of me feared that I would not be. As I lay in my mother's arms, I realized I'd been there before. When I entered our dreams, we've both seen the smoke on the mountain and the birth of myself.

And when I close my eyes, I talk to my mother.

we let no grief

In the mornings, my mother would tell me stories, both dead and alive. The mustering and withering of her voice, booming and inviting, would set me to sleep, where I'd close my eyes but still be awake.

In the great drinking days that served as the eternal fountain, things took shape and hold of us my mother would say. And I knew that

constant stream ach ing the side of mirror veiled left wonder ing right above to side gaze grazing the shine y wrought written holiday steady before weav ing enorm wild garden reeds glaring at the crossed ice melt on river side left barking hungry.

Are you hungry?

I would say yes because it was rude to say no. She would make me spam and eggs, and sometimes potatoes, using the same iron skillet to make everything. "I bet you've never had spam before?" I told her no, it was bacon or bust, and we laughed. Man, we always laughed.

And she would always boil coffee. She'd make cowboy coffee with cream

the american dream cold half full and para mount shooting roads sun belt dogs hold ing small tired lanes o months o pen nys waiting for pops pop to show shoes of feet slow ing conceal ed snow teal banks hop ping define hop define hop ing chorale straits tell dire dire dire good good good.

farther hellos

I always knew that I was given up for reasons that flooded, and flooded me—leaving me on a mountain, where I see my mother and her hand reaching down to help me up, and up, and up. How much higher, mother?

High enough to see everything.

I remember some things. I remember when I was born and hearing my brother's laugh. I remember my mother holding me and saying a Cheyenne prayer when I was sick with an ear infection. I remember my sister picking me up from the table and feeding me.

And when I dream, I remember. And when I remember, I dream, wondering if it's real—and why does it have to be.

keeping stillness

mother,

I tried to grow up fast and I failed

but I continued

to grow further into the ground while growing up and finding
the right footing and finding the right steps toward something I
knew was lost but not entirely because I was still alive finding
and finding and refusing to find refuge in

anything other than knowing God is red and still,

that was not enough for me and when I grew up

I knew the difference lay in the person you wish I would become
and it is ill to say that I was not without authority in my own
story but the memory that began to spin and spin within was lost
and lost but I remembered I would not cry when I was growing
up because I had cried enough as a child to pour my spirit into
the loss of something beyond me but Something I didn't yet
understand the keeping memory always keeping and it feels so
good around you I would always be told that love was something
that would be around me whenever I looked down

Something beyond me and therein beyond

what else is beyond

talking back to me

You know, growing up without my mother was difficult, too. I was a kind of mudflap you see on the backs of those big trucks, I was hanging on while getting beaten by the wind. When they came and got me, they didn't tell my mother I was going away. A bus pulled up in front of the school and they loaded us in. By the time it pulled out, I turned around to look and saw no one looking back.

I remember getting on the bus and being so scared. There were about ten of us. I was about eight or nine then. We were all scared. On that bus too were your aunties, your dad's sisters. Man, it was so hot. It was close to fall, and we just headed out. It got to be night and the smaller ones started crying but I didn't. I knew this would happen one day because it was happening all around us.

When we got to north dakota, we pulled in and slept. In the morning, they had about another ten kids on the bus, who were Lakota and Dakota. Man, they were just piling us in and then letting us out. By the time we got to our destination, we were so hungry. I was so hungry, I was no longer scared. That's when I cried. I cried because I knew I wouldn't get to come home. Your aunts and I were the only Cheyennes left on the bus headed to oregon.

I stayed there for a couple years until they sent us to a school in utah, the mormon place. When we got there, I got placed with a mormon family. It was hard because I was alone and alive. I didn't ever get to write home and even if I did, there wasn't a home I knew how to write back to. I didn't know my address or any other address. Your aunts stayed at that mormon camp while I stayed with this family. They were nice and they had more Native kids there. They didn't hurt us; they were quite nice to us. We all slept in one room and the older ones got their own room. By the time I turned fourteen and had gotten enough money from my job at the store, I left one morning and headed towards home. I didn't tell anyone.

By the time I got back there, everything had changed. I found out my mother was sent away to that asylum in south dakota and never came back. My brother was hid by our aunts and uncles, and had gone into the army.

And I was the only one left.

And when I got back, I wrote to my brother in Vietnam, telling him I made it home.

the end cannot be me

Before in the backstand of our existence, and even after—you did so much. My brother and sister tell me all the time that they miss you and sometimes it is enough to make me stop missing you. Your stories have been filled in with all I can remember—I am there, with you. And father.

And whenever you come to me, we take off down the same backroads with you in the driver's seat, and it feels right, this tightening of life. You tighten my life.

Imagine another life in which we are together.

let us go *mother*

let us keep going.

Her tire went flat. Her tire went flat on the bridge and the cars were about to hit her. When she came to town, her tire went flat, and then she ran out of gas. She was going to the gas station because she needed a tire, water, and gas, and she didn't have that much money so she asked the clerk at the gas station if she could get some water?—but misspoke because what she really wanted was beer but what she really needed was a tire, but she didn't have enough money to buy all three.

She had a vehicle that had no gas and a bad tire and when the clerk came outside to help her, he saw that she was an Indian wearing Indian moccasins and that's when he showed her his Indian moccasins and told her they were brand new and he liked wearing them, but she knew they were not the same as her Indian moccasins because her Indian moccasins were actually made by her Indian mother, and she told him she liked wearing them too because they went with her long Indian hair.

When she walked back to her truck, and she waited for him to fix the tire, she could tell that he really enjoyed her company because he liked hearing her Indian stories about home, but what she really couldn't tell him was that she made up most of the Indian stories because she was never told any Indian stories because she was sent away to mormon boarding school in utah when she was small and then given to a family who wanted a baby. And what he also didn't know, and she wasn't going to tell him, was that the first time she saw the great salt lake she had never felt closer to God and she never felt like Lost Tribe of Israel because Indians never get lost, but she had to tell him what he wanted to hear and so she told him a story—

As I made my way back to the desert, on
horseback, I stopped and saw a garden of
corn. The corn sprouted in front of me and
fermented.

I fermented.

I grew into myself and upward to the sky I
became blue—I returned to earth a seed and
I was planted in a frying pan.

I dance down.

After he fixed her tire for free and gave her a little gas, she started her truck
and drank the rest of the beer. Then she drove down the road and was just
over the bridge when her truck stopped again because he didn't give her
enough gas. She walked back into the same station, and when the clerk saw
her, he told her he would fill her truck up if she told him another Indian
story, and so she closed her eyes,

> my mother whisked me away and I ran to her
> again

> She sent me to the water and I did not need a
> reason to go to sleep because I must dance
> tomorrow

> I dance tomorrow and then my mother
> grabbed me

> where
> is the
> water?

where is the water.
where is the water.

Oh, she is the water.
I fall
and I ran
out of gas.

I have to
find gas I am
the engine injun.

She left the gas station, with a full tank and a brand-new tire, and drove down the same road into the same town. She pulled over at the next gas station and bought some more beer. She was so tired from driving all day from montana and she just wanted to be in gallup.

———

She had been through gallup once before, driving to phoenix for school—but this time it was not in a bus but her own car. She received a letter from her friend earlier that week who lived there. He was a Diné and sold silver jewelry on the side of Route 66. They went to carpentry school together and he asked her to come down for the summer to help him sell to tourists. After graduating, she couldn't find a lot of work in montana and needed a reason to leave. And so she did. She left with a box of matches, some cigarettes, her brother's jacket and her favorite record *Surrealistic Pillow*. It was 1969 and she told her brother she'd see him soon.

When she pulled up to her friend's house, the dogs barked. Her friend came outside and gave her a hug. Inside, she met his girlfriend and his mother, who lived with them. Over dinner, his mother told her she was heading to california to go to a rally in san francisco later that night with this group she had been meeting with. His mother showed her *Custer Died for Your Sins* and told her to read it.

"Why don't you come with me?"

"I don't have the money to go that far, but I would," she said, "and what is it for?"

Before his mother could answer, the girlfriend suggested they could sell jewelry on the way for gas money and then sell jewelry at the rally. They could probably sell the entire summer's worth.

They took a couple moments and decided to go—but first, it was time to party.

———

After his mother headed out, the three of them rode into gallup on the wheels of her Plymouth Valiant. Hitting up a bar that flew the american flag inside, she took her two-for-one special and headed for the jukebox. She put on Jefferson Airplane and summoned her friends. They stood next to a pool table with Indians wearing jackets with patches that read AMERICAN INDIAN MOVEMENT. His girlfriend saw someone who owed her money and disappeared in the crowd.

She sat and watched her friend go to the jukebox and put on a Waylon Jennings song.

"This is my song."

"I know."

She watched him go into the crowd and grab his girlfriend and the two of them begin to dance together. She remembered that dance. She caught her face in a mirrored Budweiser sign and stared at herself gently. She lit a cigarette.

———

At every gas station and rest stop, they sold jewelry. Together, they would sit in chairs next to her open car trunk with trays of jewelry on display, holding a sign that read AUTHENTIC INDIAN JEWELRY. She was tasked with talking to the tourists because he said she looked the most Indian out of everyone. And he wasn't wrong. Back then, she was looking real Bill Cody Indian.

"Are you Indian?" the white woman would ask.

"As far as I know."

"What about them?"

"They don't speak English," she would say before charging them double.

———

It was dawn when they stopped at the Grand Canyon. It wasn't her idea. He wanted to take her. "Want to watch the sunrise from the bottom of the sea?"

She nodded. "Are you experienced?"

———

Driving down the one-lane road, he parked on the side of the road and didn't wake his girlfriend. Under the coral clouds and purple mountains, they walked down a wooded path and stood together on the edge when the sun broke through. She closed her eyes.

———

When they got to monterrey, they stopped for gas. A vanload of Indians pulled into the pump and walked over. One guy, who wore a bandana and braids, was smoking a cigarette. He handed her a picture of Geronimo out of his pocket from a pack of, what looked like, trading cards.

"I'm not Apache, I'm Cheyenne. Do you have a Little Wolf one?" she asked.

"I don't know who that is. We're out of Sitting Bull and Red Cloud, all we have is Geronimo."

She took Geronimo and turned it over. On the back, it read RED POWER. She put it in her pocket.

"He's my favorite anyways. You want some jewelry?"

———

Later that morning, they arrived in san francisco and didn't know where to go.

"Where do you think this place is?" he asked. She rolled down the window and heard drums.

"Follow the drums," she said. So they did.

On the street corner, an Indian woman was holding a sign. He asked her where the powwow was and she said the powwow was everywhere. Then she pointed to the next block. Turning onto the street, they saw as many Indians as they'd ever seen; it looked like the Old World and New World in one. And she was so confused. *Why so many Indians?*

———

They parked the car and followed the crowd, when they realized they were in the middle of a march. They cut into an alley where they found the powwow grounds. There was a stage set up in the middle of the arena and food vendors all around. Natives everywhere, walking around in traditional regalia, AIM regalia and military uniforms. The bleachers were full and there were campsites of tents and teepees in the distance. They could hear the march in the streets as they felt the sun on their skin.

They were hungry and walked toward the food stands when they found his mother handing out brochures by a water stand.

"You made it!" she said, catching each of them in long hugs. "Are you guys hungry? How was your journey?"

"Is that a bandana on your head?"

She led them through the crowd to where she made camp, toward a circle of drum groups on stage. There was a man standing by a microphone. This man was Indian and when he spoke, he sounded like Chief Seattle.

When he began, everyone started clapping. She looked around and saw the National Guard. He said that grand entry would begin at noon and go until the moon landing later that night. But she didn't know there was a moon landing that night. *What moon landing?* As the drums got louder, the man got louder and he answered her question—

It is an honor to speak here tonight. As many of you know, I am a member of the American Indian Movement, from the Minneapolis Chapter. It is so good to see so many Indians in one place. Many of you may know who we are or what we do. Some may not. We are of a different sort. We are not silent. We are here to fight for you and fight for our people back home. Our people, who have lived on this land since time immemorial. Our people, who have the most entitled birthright to the land beneath our feet. However, as this country has said, it is not only ours to walk on, it is also *theirs*.

As you know, as Indian people, we have long been forgotten by this america, but we have never been so feared. This government is proving that our presence is power, and with that power, we will no longer be denied our fundamental right to live and breathe on this land we have called home for more than a millennia. We will be silent no more.

We are the first americans and we cannot vote. We are the first americans and we cannot fish in our own rivers. We are the first americans and we cannot hunt on our own land. We are the first americans and we cannot worship freely. We are the first americans and we don't have electricity in our homes.

We *are* the first americans but this government does not even consider us americans.

Today, we call on this government to restore our land.

Today, we call on this government to honor our treaties and grant us our fishing and water rights.

Today, we call on this government to abolish the Bureau of Indian Affairs and give us our full sovereignty so we may become the most self-determined.

Tonight, when that man walks on the moon, he will not only be the first american to walk on the moon, but the first *real* american to walk on the moon: the only *true* american. But many of you did not know this. Many of you did not know that tonight an Indian will be on the moon. This is because the government has hidden it from us. But ask yourselves, why is the government hiding his identity from us, its citizens? Why is the government hiding his identity from us, its original people? Why does this government not want the world to know that he is an Indian? My friends, it is because this country refuses to see Indian people here on earth, as humans—humans that are not of the past, but capable of finding new frontiers.

We will be idle no more. As the Soviets sent their Russian dog to orbit the stars over ten years ago, tonight, the federal government will send its american dog to orbit the stars. Tonight, we will watch the first man walk on the moon and he will be an Indian man. And what glory this will bring to this country and to humanity. For many years, our ancestors have told us not to touch the stars before it is our time. But why does america want to touch the stars? Why does this country want to touch the moon? It is because they want to claim it for themselves.

I want to remind everyone here that once this Indian walks on the moon tonight, the world will see him only as a human—even if this country does not. As of today, we will not allow this government to continue this cover so as to hide the truth from the world. Remember what our ancestors believed so deeply they died for. Do not surrender for there will be a better tomorrow. The world now knows. And we know.

Today, we are walking into the future and we will be

silent no more. The Red Movement has begun.

america never looked for us

I forget my name and it turns me gold

canned heat in winter is warm
when I find you and
listen to
all we've become.

can you dream in color
if you were not born in color?

you once told me we could never separate
being Native from
the original

big migration
into
you're in america now.

listening to stay

In albuquerque, I asked this guy at the gas station for a lighter. He was this Navajo who had this red bandana on and looked like your uncle. He had this big gash on his pant-leg and when I looked down, I realized he didn't have a leg at all. I said, oh man what happened to you? He said he just lost it to diabetes and that it was now probably in some museum somewhere. He laughed and I did too. You have to really be careful with those archaeologists and scientists because they'll come around here and start asking about some of our cemeteries and then go off and dig us up. So we don't tell anyone. Half of our young people don't even know where the cemeteries are, only their grandparents do and that's good. That's good. We have to protect them. Sometimes, you'll see those people on the side of the road with their shovels digging and we'll have to run them off. I wonder what will happen to me and my bones.

driving around looking for you

through the light brought into this world wherever could the darkness be whenever you talk to me in Cheyenne I can't understand your words but I know what you are saying was it ever this unclear subtle prompting setting me and you apart at least when prompted I see the Indian in you much more than I see the one in me and you have long hair, oh it is darker oh but I am dark too riddled with shadowed humor that would bait the consciousness of you and ask why

only as old as we've been told

mother,

you were always curt when someone asked you questions. You had a way you answered them. When the doctor asked what you were going to name your first daughter at your only clinic appointment, you didn't know. You said you never knew until the time was right. And was it ever right?

I never saw the world you did. You had a life that was met with the mark of the Indian verb. Action. Indian Action. You were an Indian in AIM, where you would bead on the bus to a rally. You would wake up, brush your hair, put on your denim jacket and become the 1970s cowboy everyone wanted to be. But you never took it too far. You'd tell me that that was a time when both cowboys and Indians wanted to be Indians and ride around on horses with long hair—but only Indians are Indians. Still, I haven't worn a cowboy hat but brother's favorite team is the Cowboys.

You spent your life remembering our past. There is a picture of you at Sand Creek with a shovel, finding the remains of our grandparents who fell that day, and at the Smithsonian, where you're standing next to the Natural History Museum days before they returned our people's remains. You were action.

You remembered. You fought. You spoke.

You are the reason

I always listened to You told me whole stories in pieces and
sometimes I would get lost in the way you speak. Your hushed
tones and soft inflection had me listening closely always afraid I
wouldn't hear or understand. But I always did. From the pieces of
memory I have left I have made your stories whole

/ mythos

little one

your birth and life with me and your existence after have blurred into each other and when I think of you and your family, I wish you were with me and mine. Your life has been lost to me. We know what we have seen and hearing about your life growing up with your family has made me wish we lived it together and after meeting you

I know we both

                                                            wish

when you were born, you looked like your dad but I gave you my name. You were tiny and brown with a small birthmark on your back that I didn't pay much attention to because I had one too. You didn't either, until you were older and I told you. When your preschool teacher asked me if I had noticed the bruise on your back I said no, because it is wasn't a bruise, but a birthmark. I then had to go to the pediatrician and ask him to write a letter to prove the mark wasn't a bruise. In the letter, the doctor said that Native children have that mark on their back, the Mongolian birthmark, but the school was still skeptical. I decided to take you out of that city preschool and bring you back home because I didn't want any trouble. The reservation was where you needed to be.

When your father and I decided to have you, we knew we weren't ready, but we also knew we had to give life where life was due—and though it wasn't an easy birth, you were an easy child. You were quiet and you learned all the things I was supposed to teach you. Your ABC's, your 123's. I taught you Cheyenne because you wanted to learn and you always had trouble with the long *u* sounds but that was only because you didn't like the way they felt in your throat. You grew up by yourself because we lived outside of town. On weekends, you and your father would watch tv and go to Denny's. In middle school, you ran track and cross-country. You were so good at running that sometimes you would gloat, which I had never seen you do before. You were always humble and the times when I would get after you, it was only because you had too many friends. I always told you that to keep a friend, you had to be a friend. And while you had many friends, sometimes I didn't know if they had you. I can't remember when you first started going out with your friends, but I remember the time you went out on your father's birthday. You said you were going to celebrate. How could you celebrate without your father?

The next week, that same house next to ours had cop cars all around it because a girl had gone missing from it and I remember you running home from school, scared.

In high school, you were class president, and some students took to calling you tribal president. You thought that was so funny because one day you really did want to be tribal president. You always took dancing very seriously and always spoke to your grandparents in Cheyenne. They loved that about you. When your aunt Charla would come over, she would talk to you in Cheyenne. You loved her so much, and she loved you. Sometimes, when you were real little, you would call her sister, but I would always remind you that she was your auntie. One day in the kitchen, you took your first steps to her. She was so happy and when she picked you up, you gave her the biggest hug. I still remember that picture.

You were always your father's favorite because you looked like him. When you graduated preschool, your father asked you what you wanted to be when you got older, and you said hungry.

We laughed and later that year, for Halloween, you went as a bottle of ketchup.

I remember how excited you were to be going to college. You had tried to run track at the state university but then decided that you wanted to go to tribal college. You wanted to study history because I had; as you said, that was where the real knowledge was. I remember you studying for that test and getting into the college. We had a big dinner for you, and afterward you went out with your friends.

When I was that age, I had already met your dad. We would go out all the time and got into a couple car crashes together. We would always cruise around and go swim in the spring during the summer. I was there when that eighteen-wheeler caught the hills on fire and your dad and uncle and I helped put it out. We were always together until your dad left. You were so young you don't remember, but I would hold you when you and I were both sick, waiting for someone to hold us. It got cold that winter and I would wrap you up and put you in the chair by the stove. We would go walking up the hills and pray. I remember one time, we took off to billings and you were all bundled up in the front seat, in your auntie's arms, and got the biggest diaper either of us had ever seen. We had to stop on the side of the road to change it. You were just laughing. Always laughing.

When your dad came back, he brought a lot of money. He had been building things in new mexico and arizona, making seats and seatbelts, and welding chairs together. We went to billings and bought you so many baby clothes. Your favorite color was red, so your father and I would buy you so many red things. We once bought you a red nose, for Christmas, to look like a reindeer. We loved you so much and you loved us. I remember you so clearly, you in your red shoes, and me in mine.

will we return?

One man gets sick, another man gets sick, another man gets sick, another man gets sick, they are huddled and have no water and the sickness is upon them— it is hunger, it is tire; it is cold. The stupor is beyond them, and they look to their periphery and see they're not on the plains, but surrounded by wooden pillars so tall, in every direction, beyond their easy climb, guarded by men on horseback; military men with rifles. How do they leave?

———

Pockets in a pouch for tobacco worn across my neck, pouches of dried meat palmed by my son beneath his clothes, pockets in my horse's pack, pockets in the coat that carried the sickness I can feel but cannot name, and I look up to ask my son, "do you think the horse can feel it too?"

———

It is snowing and I am cold, and my skin itches, and my hands make their way to both my back and my legs, sometimes at the same time, and it does not help because while my clothes are thick, it is the fever that keeps me freezing. My face begins to itch and I look ahead and hope for more snow so I cannot feel my face.

———

The bluffs appear beside the frozen river and I lead the horse through a clearing I once walked with my own father when we hunted.

My son is bundled next to the clothes he did not touch. I offered him the

31

coat I found at the abandoned campsite; but he wouldn't take it because he said I needed a thicker covering.

I was wearing the coat when my arm began to itch. And now, I ignore the itch because I know it will spread.

I cannot remember how long it takes to get to the next camp. Is it days?—weeks?

It is afternoon; and I cannot remember how long it has been since we left our camp.

I tell my son to lean into the wind.

———

I say a prayer when my feet stumble. I need to make it to the edge of the winding bluffs before nightfall so we can build a fire on the safe side of the mountains.

As our pace strays, I talk to my son and remind him of his name, his strength, our people's strength, our people's hope, and my hope for him. I tell him how his grandfather suffered from the same sicknesses that we have no name for and that our journey will continue in the next world; and there will be no more sickness. I tell him not to touch me. I tell him to remember the river, the clearing, and the path from where we came. I tell him to remember. I begin to fly.

i don't have dream words

My father was quiet and tall. And big. A beautiful face. Rough. Since he left the army, he always kept his hair short, wore jeans, white shirts, and wore an OU ball cap. He was very spiritual and a ceremonial man. He'd sit with his wrists crossed over his chest and his legs crossed over his ankles. And he'd speak softly.

My father had the power to bend time. He could be everywhere you needed him to be, without cue. He simply manifested.

I do not know where or how he met my mother. I never asked. I am sure he tries to forget while my mother tries to remember. They had all of us kids one year apart and all in the summer. He loved my mother and my mother loved him, but she never said so. He didn't talk unless he was telling stories. I remember him laughing, but very quietly. I remember him listening, even when he was speaking. I remember him coughing.

After my father left my mother and went to oklahoma, my father spent the majority of my life looking and looking and looking for me. He looked for me in my sister, he looked for me in my brother, he looked for me in my mother, he looked for me in the phone book, and when he found me, he looked for himself in me.

Before I met him, I only knew him in stories told by my sister and mother. Stories of how my father would disappear for months, even years, and live alone or with his cousins, either in montana or in oklahoma, and would come back to the reservation in scattered currents. And when he did return, he would always bring my brother and sister new shoes. New shoes for growing feet. Sometime, when my brother and sister were teenagers, he stopped visiting.

You know your mom would hold her fists closed when she'd come around me and my hands would always be up. She was a tough lady, your mom. I didn't know she had you. I'd just moved back to

oklahoma and one of your uncles congratulated me when I was walking to the gas station. I thought he was congratulating me for winning a scratch-off I had, so I kept walking. I didn't know till later when I called the house and your sister told me and your mom got mad. Thought I was going to go up there and take you. I would have, I just couldn't. Your mom was angry at me and every time I went up there to try and meet you, she wouldn't let me. She'd hide you. I never saw you.

We didn't talk for a long time after that. But, that next time I went up there determined, and she told me she sent you to texas and that she didn't put my name on your birth certificate so I couldn't do anything about it. I just gave up and went back home. I never talked to your mom after that. Not until you came back.

spinning air

When my father was seven, he and his cousin would drive around el reno, oklahoma. You didn't have to have a license then, you just had to be able to see over the steering wheel. Whenever they got pulled over by the police, they ran.

When my father was seventeen, he and his cousin were thrown in for driving into the Depot on Halloween. *We pinned a guy up on the wall and his legs were kicking.* He mimed kicking legs with his fingers. *He was fine—we just backed up.*

After a year, they were transferred to the state prison, where they were locked up for two more years. My father said he and my uncle got in with the Indian gang—but not just with any Indian gang, the Cheyenne and Arapaho Indian Gang.

   That many Cheyennes, huh?

   Well, between your uncle and I there were about three of us.

———

Whenever I would visit my father, he would pat the chair where he wanted me to sit. Waiting for each other to speak meant for long silences—but we were comfortable. Sharing this newfound time with my family, I realized that the way I postured, carried myself, walked, sat down—all the characteristics I didn't share with my parents—I shared with him and my mother. We walked the same, hunched, and heavy stepped. Flat, but heel first.

Later one night, we were sitting on the porch. My father in a folding chair and I on the step, the wind the loudest voice between us. We crossed our legs together at the ankles. Sharing silences—we both listened to everything—the air through the door, the highway cars driving past, the neighbor's car doors shutting, and I to his sigh.

Feeling the cool weather, watching the wind, he leaned into me and said *it takes a long time to stay here.*

part of the reason, the reason for the ruggedness is that I am
cold and I don't have any money, so I keep this oven open, like
this. Hopefully it won't catch fire, or else I'll really be warm.
Your brother is in the back cutting up a deer. I don't miss the
winters here. I don't miss the cold, but I do miss the summers. It
gets too hot in oklahoma. I got another house down there, in
oklahoma. Your uncle is staying there, looking after it, but when
I get down there after the snow is gone, I may just stay there.
The oven can't keep me warm forever. I just ran out of coffee
and can't make it down the Depot. Could you get some for me?

I nod my head.

I bet it doesn't get this cold in texas. I went to texas once. I
drove through with a group of us to gather parts after that
shuttle exploded over the sky. Remember that shuttle? The
Columbia? I headed down that way to pick up parts for the
government. The closest I ever got to being an astronaut, but
with a bad headache. All that pollen in the springtime down
there, it messed up my head. I tried to go to IHS to get
medicine for the pollen, but there wasn't one down there in
texas. There must not be that many Indians in texas.

I shake my head.

I got that feeling. You know when you're the only Indian

somewhere, and you can just feel it. I felt that way when I was in the army. Look around and you're the only one.

I nod my head.

I tried to find you while I was there. I tried to find you. I knew you were in texas somewhere, but your mother never told me where, so everywhere I stopped, I looked for you. I didn't know your family's last name, so I just described you from the last picture I had of you. I used to keep it in my wallet, but then I lost that wallet. So I'd describe it from memory. Said you were about this tall, and you wore this shirt, this red shirt. Your hair was this long. But then I realized I was describing no one. I was describing everyone. Hey everyone, I'd say, have you seen a four-foot girl, she's got brown hair and brown skin. She's my daughter, anyone seen her? And here you are now, about the same size. Maybe a little taller.

city thirst

The sun had been going down for quite some time when she rushed into the house to grab some things. He was drinking a beer.

"Hey, where you going?" he asked.

"seattle. My brother has papers he needs to sign. I have to go find him."

"Well shit, you need someone to drive? I have gas money."

They grabbed the cooler, the Pampers bag, some blankets and a bottle and headed out the door to the car. It was summer.

She asked, "Who has the baby?"

———

When they pulled up at my aunt's house, she told them that the baby was inside sleeping. So, they walked in and grabbed him.

As they were about to head out of town, they drove by my aunt Charla's house to see if they could borrow her car because she had a nicer car. When they pulled up, she said, "Well shit, you need someone to drive? I have gas money."

So then, it was my aunt, my mother, and my father heading west toward seattle. The whole way they kept going back to that cooler. My father didn't even think to ask what these papers were for because he was along for the ride—and at that time, anyways, he was too afraid of my mom to ask.

So, they drove through bozeman, then boise, then spokane, and then seattle.

My mother made a basket out of blankets around my brother and put him in the backseat between the cooler and my aunt. The whole drive he never cried. He never made a sound. My aunt and my father took turns holding him throughout the night. And at daylight the next morning, he woke up and laughed.

My brother needed to laugh.

When they got outside seattle, they pulled up at a gas station to ask where the Seattle Indian Center was.

When they got to the Center, they asked everyone around if they knew my uncle but no one did. They went into the men's hostel, asking the front desk if they knew any Cheyenne people there. When the clerk pointed to a couple men outside smoking a cigarette, my mother handed my brother to my father and walked toward the door. When my uncle saw my mother, he put out his cigarette and gave her a hug. They talked for a long time while my father looked for a vending machine. My uncle wasn't sober then and wore a red bandana around his head. He liked shirts with pearl buttons and cowboy boots. He signed the papers and said he had to go to work.

———

On the way back to montana, my father finally asked my mother what those papers were for.

She said my uncle had a baby who was just born that he didn't know about and needed to get these papers signed so the little one could have his name and blood quantum.

"Boy or girl?" he asked.

"I don't know."

He looked down at my brother who was awake in his arms. My brother started laughing.

40

when quiet tangle speaks

I was nervous around your grandfather, experiencing the wildness and stillness of his laydown when he would sit there. He never spoke, and when he left, he'd leave for long days at a time. He went to boarding school when he was a child. And when he got out of there, he moved to oklahoma to be with his mother. I joined the army when I was old enough to leave the house. I was the oldest and I watched my sisters go into group homes in and out of montana. It was a rough time for all of us. A child never has money and my sisters were sent to utah. They didn't know when their birthdays were because my mom never told them.

If you don't know your birthday, do you ever get older?

We were all small, interred crumbs, uncertain crumbs, unsure crumbs, interrupted crumbs. It was better to go away than to stay.

I never asked my sisters what it was like being raised in utah. Who were they when they were there? What was their life like? When they'd come back and visit in the summers, we would be together like no time had passed. They'd tell me it was all concrete where they were, all birthday cake and no trees like there were here. After mom died, they stopped visiting because they couldn't stay with our father who would disappear. I got sent to oklahoma to stay with my aunt, until I was fifteen and decided to join the army. I wonder what my mom would say about that, joining the army, fraternizing with the enemy. That's her silver bracelet over there on the counter. When you leave here don't forget to take that bracelet with you and remember to fix the clasp.

i lost all the nights

Once in the winter, my aunt Charla was in downtown helena. She caught a ride with her friend the night before from the reservation.

When she woke up in the car on the way to helena, she asked her friend where they were going.

When she first woke up in the car, she didn't know where she was, but then remembered the house party the night before and guessed she probably told her friend, "Drop me off in helena, I got an aunt up there."

She knew our aunt lived there, but she didn't know where, exactly.

When she got to helena, her friend dropped her off near the downtown bus station because it had a payphone, then kept driving on to boise.

Charla checked her pockets for money, and thankfully, pennied up about $13 in loose bills and change—left over from buying the night before. It was the first of the month. She said she called my father, but he wasn't home. He was probably out doing the same thing.

The winter sky reminded her of night and she needed a place to stay. She knew she could sleep at the YMCA, the homeless shelter, or the emergency room at the hospital. She knew she could get food from the homeless shelter, or some church because they like to help Indians.

One time before, she got stranded in seattle for a couple weeks without money and found her way back home by hitching a ride with some Salish at a bus stop because they shared one cousin on her mother's side. It's like that too, we're all related in some way. She bounced from rez to rez all the way back to ours.

That night, she took off toward the nearest casino she remembered going to last time she was in helena.

When she got there, she saw a group smoking outside and she asked for a cigarette. She then asked if anyone knew where the nearest homeless shelter was.

Because it was wintertime, she knew the homeless shelter was probably almost full—especially at that hour. So, she headed out and tried to keep herself hyped, knowing it may just be a longer night than it was day.

She called my father again, and he answered that time. He told her he didn't remember where their aunt stayed, but it was somewhere on the west side. He wired her some money and told her to stay warm.

She said it was too far a walk to try to make it over there at that hour and she was going to stay at the homeless shelter.

But when she got there, the shelter was full. All she was wearing was a cotton jacket. She walked around until she saw a group of Indians huddled next to each other in an alley with blankets.

She walked up and said she was Cheyenne and then someone asked what her last name was. An older man spoke up and said, "I'm Cheyenne too." It was one of our distant cousins.

She nodded and asked him if she could take a swig of the Sailor Jerry he was holding. He offered her part of his blanket and a cigarette as they both leaned into the wind. They kept passing the bottle of Sailor Jerry back and forth until they went to sleep.

She said she woke up to the nudge of this lady sitting next to her, telling her to wake up our cousin. She tried, but he wouldn't move. His head was down, and his back was stiff. When my aunt nudged him again, her push sent him sideways. That was when she saw his eyes—unblinking, unresponsive, and glazed over with frost. Frozen tears. He was clutching his fists.

When life hits you like that, you'll look in the mirror and see what it's done.

rearview

no watch on
your wrist
but I ask you
what time it is.
—suntime
I catch your
smile before
you catch mine.

all air going north and a walk outside

My father noticed my distrust of the landscape as I saw it through his life. america never looked for us at all, but I'm better with you, I told my father. I don't know if he heard me.

One lit candle, after another, on the table in a two-bedroom house with a muddy driveway. Fifty years ago, his own mother sitting in a rocking chair near the stove, watching him play outside from the window. Corn and potatoes for dinner.

His mother scratches her hand until it bleeds and asks the catholic priest for forgiveness. Forgiveness from who? And at thirty, she dies from diabetes.

No concrete better, no marble statue erected in anyone's honor except at the catholic church—a saint—when I saw my father's cedar coffin laying at the front of the church, beneath the priest's hand. It made me feel small and raging. But at who?

Cheyenne songs en masse and catholic prayers—ideas that don't work out in the long run—in a church that was built to resemble a teepee. Burning cedar near a cedar box.

I look at my feet. Black heels and a black dress. I am wearing black, in a catholic church attending my father's funeral. Walking out to the burial site.

It is cold outside. And the ground is so frozen, my heels do not sink into the clay.

Father, is it too late to tell you, when mother called me every Christmas and every birthday—did you know that I wished for you?

And the last time you called me, you said it was so cold that your chest hurt, and it was this cold.

seeing by night

It is summer and I have come back to Lame Deer to spend time with you. My family, you are perfect as I let you be. You are as brown as me; and I thank all there is to thank—mostly my god—but also the gods I let be and the ones I do not.

I know the way to the reservation.

I drive to the west side of Lame Deer. I haven't visited in many years, but something stains familiar each time. I avoid the potholes and rogue dogs. It is beautiful, as far as the headlights show, and beyond—and I do want to see beyond.

I pull up to your mother's house and I see you standing in the yard talking to your sister.

I walk to the door and you smile at me
as you do.

measure of life through light

i stare at stars and she stares at me

the dream is dreamt

Riding the smallest mornings into a two-bedroom house in a place that is cold in the summer will smother you.

My sister is a knowledge keeper and she knows it. Even when she takes off and forgets to grab her jacket because she is too tired and can't remember the last time she ate, she knows it.

The alley-oop of night to cold is antiseptic to warmth inside the house. The weather is always present, and her depths are spent. My sister told me about the time her girlfriend turned thirty and being her little sister, I listened.

Her girlfriend cried because it was her birthday and she had no one to celebrate with because her closest friends and some of our cousins never made it to thirty and it was lonely being the only one left to celebrate, and although I didn't understand, I listened. It is lonesome to celebrate your life at a wake.

That year, I went to Six Flags, and she told me that is Six Flags over You, and Six Flags over Me. Being raised apart from her for half my life halved our lives.

When she was young, and I was young, you could not tell our laughs apart. So, whenever she was laughing, I was laughing too.

Riding the biggest roller coaster, I remember grabbing her hand and thinking that if she were to let go, I would disappear. The grip from her hand was the only thing holding me within myself while I was flying

65 mph through the air on a metal track. And when she let go, I never felt more alone. I held my head to my chest and counted down from ten before I woke up.

After waking, I touted my dream in the kitchen. I had a dream where we were at Six Flags, I told her, and when we got on the biggest ride at the park, we were going down together. When we neared the bottom, you let go of my hand and I kept going down and down. She laughed. *What is Six Flags?*

I told her I wished that we were raised together. That when the time and place was decided in another life, we would be born and raised together. I would hear her first vowel, and she would hear mine. Like twins, we would be inseparable. She heard this, she sat down at the table and grabbed my hand. I told her not to let go, or else we both would disappear.

When my sister decided to leave home, it was not because she wanted to. She told me it was because she needed to. The cold nights and permanent pinpricks were things I would never know. She told me of times when our older brother would offer her his last bite of food and she would always say yes. Her youth was that of an Indian on a reservation. A place where I would not be.

Here was where our worlds collided. We didn't share a history, but we had the present. She held my hand. And being a younger sister, in awe of her older sister, I waited for her to tell me more.

who's to say whether the future ever saw us together. I knew you were my phantom sibling, somewhere.

Mom never talked about you much. And when she did, she always said you were good. And were you?

Do you look like me?

I, too, made a series of missteps and misalignments being . . . being here. Being there. It's hard being here. It was okay until I got with that councilman's daughter in high school and he started telling everyone about us so I dropped out and left.

When I asked you for Western Union last week, I meant could you send me some money so that I could buy a bus ticket. I didn't think you could buy real joy through a seat on the back of a bus heading north in the snow, but you can when you're leaving this place. I camp by the river when it's hot at night, and on the west side of the mountain when it's cold. The night of your birthday, I was playing hide and seek with the cops, but they never find me by the river because I can sense them.

I got this way with cops. I've just about got the sound of their cars and their steps down. I can always tell how far away they are. This side of my head hurts when it gets too cold. I think it's my ears. They send the sharpest pains into my neck here and my eyes start to water and get dried out. It's all connected, you see.

I met my girlfriend on that bus before she went left to boise and I went right to billings. One of the worst feelings is telling a lover you don't really care about the things they do, when really you do.

I always worried about you growing up, and I think Mom did too, but she didn't say. We were kids. We wanted to know what you looked like, and what you were doing, but she wouldn't tell. She wouldn't say. We may not have known a lot, but we knew about you.

She would say, only we know what we've seen.

make a new millennia

last night i dreamed in color

riding scars

burying us carrying
us up down

to fathered destination

with a beautiful bow
is what we were

told you
grab sunday's imagination
of beholding

and beholding tries its best
to party

under an illuminated same

Negative thinking lies at my sister's feet before she kicks it away to get up and go to work. She misses and accidentally hits the puppy asleep beside her favorite scarf. She just got a house on the reservation and is going to her job at the local bank. On her way out, she grabs the last diet coke in the refrigerator. It is 9am on her last day of work.

The bank is the only remaining white institution on the reservation and tomorrow they will close it down. Tomorrow, they will do away with her job, and they will do away with all the money left on the reservation. Tomorrow, the Tribe will return to the days before money and live for themselves again.

The council decided long ago, before my sister was born, that someday the time would come to reject the white man's designs and return to the Tribe's. It was decided that that day would be tomorrow.

My sister grabs a coffee at the Trading Post and wonders what will happen—will this store even remain? Despite her uncertainty, she trusts the Tribe enough to keep her fed forever.

———

Years before, my sister graduated with an MBA from business school in billings and found a white job at a bank and a white dog at the shelter and a white girlfriend at the coffee shop and a nice apartment with white walls next to the nicest hotel downtown. And she lived there very comfortably, until she was called to come home.

Her escape into love had given her new self-esteem. But being with her girlfriend also led to social isolation and intolerance from her family and Tribe. So, when she returned to the reservation with nothing but the dog and the diploma, the Tribe welcomed her back and she got a job at the bank.

———

At work, my sister chats up the new clerk who was hired from the same college, then leans over and tells the next clerk, *she's hot.* Despite having a beautiful face that men noticed, and all the trouble it brought her, she was quite alright loving her lovers, even if the Tribe wasn't.

At the end of the day, my sister returns to her home on the road that runs between her and her mother's. She built a new house with the money she saved up in billings and gave the rest of her earnings to other families so they could build their own houses. Happiness is the only truth.

When my sister wakes the next morning, although nothing seems different, everything has changed. Now, it is time for her to start living as the people did before anything she's ever known.

———

Without paper money circulating throughout the reservation, the Tribe had to find another means of currency that was easily distributable. Its clarity and efficiency were missed, at first. The boys discarded their Jordan slides and the girls found no use for their Adidas laces once winter came. The cheap durability of these once-treasured goods ultimately proved them worthless.

It wasn't until the schools and churches were repurposed into housing and community centers that the children started listening to their teachers. Parents were now engaged and present—not because they wanted to be, but because they had to be. Bars were no longer open and all they had brought was poured back into the fire. And when the parents told their children stories, the grandparents listened. And when the children listened to their grandparents, they were reminded of a time before the church came and the money.

Over time, the children began rejecting the image of god and fully understood the true genesis of their people—at the mountain—in the stars. Ma'heo'e. As a result of this understanding, the bad news of christianity was banished to the empty mines of the neighboring coal power plant, where it lies this day.

In the absence of the christian church, my sister—on the arm of her new girlfriend, the clerk at the bank—was welcomed into the community. A union made of two Cheyenne women was understood to be sacred because Cheyenne women are sacred. They live together in their new home.

Once dogma of christianity was forgotten, the tribal spirit began to heal. Communal ceremonies, band-kinship systems, and Cheyenne familial laws were reinstated and followed.

All the things of the old world became new again. The time was rife with new spirit.

———

The people understood that, with time, everyone would adjust to this new way of life. The council deferred to the people and a new demand for culture created a new value that was contrived from the days of old, when men and women would give their labor for their family and community and become valuable citizens of their living nation.

Past circuses and past lives would occasionally disrupt the Tribe. But now the Tribe knew what to do. Armed with the knowledge of history, the Tribe avoided the familiar traps and people became wealthy in each other. New stories were born—stories that held the same truths, but included the cautionary tales of past alienation, war, and sickness.

It was the stories that brought us back to life and kept us alive forever and ever.

And a small glimpse into infinity would find my sister helping helping helping and loving loving loving having been loved.

[somewhere] and kept

abovescape
you say *how*
did I get
this high
to see the ruin
ed limbs tear
ing the memory taken
from a place through
the breaking of
our perfect whole
who am I
sister? if a
part

i watch you but you do not watch me

We sit at the table and you tell me that you have a magic jacket that will take us somewhere we do not know. I ask you if it is a Pendleton jacket, and you tell me no, this jacket is cosmic. It is the warmest jacket in the world. And it is used.

Nowadays, you speak in riddles, and sometimes I don't know what you are saying. But as your little sister, I'll always listen to you. I know when our cousin drowned in the river, you did not have the voice to say any words out loud, but I want you to know that they were still all the right ones. Your words gave me the hope to continue, dropping the red sweater in the dirt hole, which you told me was holy dirt. *Remember that jacket?* The jacket that our mother got you when you were really little and forgot how small you really were. It's that jacket. Still big enough to cover your world.

We sit at the table and you tell me you have a magic jacket that will take us somewhere we do not know. You say that you have seen the sewing of this jacket, and it isn't strong enough to take us both. You tried before when I was really small—before you knew me. I tell you I still don't remember, and you tell me to stop repeating myself. You try to explain— it's too easy,

her red sweater's lost
but she will fly
again

i chat with god and it feels so good

i kneel

our cousin is trying to commit suicide but we both know the balcony is
too shallow

nothing is escapable cousin

she asks me if the first word ever spoken was silent

if we were white our drink
would mean something different

we were given forever
time and never had one drink
nothing is escapable

mom said it all goes downhill from here
and sometimes it's good

was the first word ever spoken, silent?

the weight of my
existence the weight
of my existence i dirty
a room with my existence.

i wish to proceed

there's nothing to eat
i could eat an afternoon

we are almost out of groceries because i have used all the salmon
the dogs barked

so muffled dark and low
a tv on black

this corruption of flesh
this (attuned, affixed, a must)

trip with me

i am a fish in the air

this is what kafka really meant when he wished to be a red indian

Every now and again, you examine the ground before you, very jerkily, because you are not on a racing horse, but behind the wheel of a chevy malibu on a dirt road on a reservation. You are leaning with the wind because you want your hair to cover your eyes, so you could pretend you were on a racing horse. You are instantly alert because your brother, who is driving, could hit a racing horse who may be crossing the road before you. You are not wearing any spurs—you do not need any reins. The racing horse will take you to a place where the land that was once gone is now back and your horse's neck and head are actually yours.

the blood on your shirt is mine

They drank ten beers today. He drank two in the morning, and then when she woke up, they drank eight more.

They drank ten beers today, and tonight, they are going to party.

He sees his friend's van drive up the road.

She falls asleep.

———

He drank a case of beer today. He drank half in the morning, and when she woke up, they drank

the other half.

They drank a case of beer today, and tonight, they are going to cruise around.

She sees her little nephew wearing one velcro shoe, asking to watch tv. She tells him his older

brother pawned the tv.

He runs outside to play.

———

She climbs into the back of the van and searches for the watch she dropped in the car last night.

She knows the search will be fruitless, but she's drunk enough to care.

Their friends wear down the red dirt road that takes them across the plains into the nearest town.

Rugged town rugged road rugged people.

I look out the window.

We are flying.

hover our grey

My older brother used to say that he was one thousand nine hundred and ninety-two years old, until I told him that was just his birth year. I would tell him I was a 20th-century orphan, always feeling that the rocking horse beneath me might turn to dust, into mud, and I would rise on real horseback, craving the taste of dead meat. But we were both the sandwiched generation, born with a steady anger about the world we had been given. We always needed each other. And we always had each other, within ourselves.

His die cast on fast times, and he lived fast times on this land, this land where we've all been born since time immemorial.

hustle the roads

brother
muted edge

who carries life
of war
what is
of ours

tiny tears in a totem
a marched
generation

turn the rocking horse to mud
the horse to meat.

driveway dreams

My brother and I joke about how we can see the future. The future can be as big and bright as we want, I say. So long as we don't have standards.

One night at dinner, I ask him if he saw himself born.

He slurps his soup and says he always knew he would be Cheyenne. Moments later, he jumps up and grabs his bottled water to pour on the dogs who are fighting outside.

"How is it being here?"

"If I had the choice again, don't know if I'd want to live here, in this house. It's hard getting housing here, but I wish I didn't get this house. Too many cracks."

It's conversations like these that drive me inward and within. Who am I, but an outsider, asking her older brother about his life when I should know.

Sitting at the family table, I take in a stained ceiling and some loose cracks in the door. "How was it growing up here?"

"I don't know . . . it just was. It is. It was rough sometimes. I used to be about your size and got beat up a lot but now that I'm bigger, it's better. I have friends here to make it better, too. That guy you met last night, he's my best friend. He makes it the best it can be. I grew up here so you know, it's home." He shrugs. "I always like those tower buildings like they got in cities, like where you're at in texas, sky high, no railroad trestles around. But they also scare me. Like wildfires. Here, the wildfires take all they want from us. The trees I grew up with have gone and burnt up."

To tell him sorry is useless because I don't know what he is feeling. I try to imagine what it must have looked like before. Green and wide. It is now brown and black.

"Trees everywhere. It's those trees I miss. The big tall ones. Everywhere. Last summer, I had a friend drive up that mountain on this dirt road and hit a stump and roll down about a hundred feet. But when he hit those big trees down below"—my brother folds his hand like he is cupping water— "it had his car like this, nestled, cradled. He ended up climbing out the back window, but that car is still there in that tree. Those limbs have grown into it now."

I shake my head. It's all I know what to do when we talk like this. I don't know the right things to feel. I want to hug him like I would a friend but we aren't friends, we're siblings and we've just met.

"Another one of my friends, when we were about fifteen, headed out that way, walking along the highway with all those trees on that curve, and one of those big semitrucks didn't see him, I mean the driver says he didn't see him, but he . . ." My brother softly claps his hands together and shakes his head.

I shake my head with him. "I'm sorry brother." I look down.

"I'm glad you're here." He gets up and goes to the kitchen to make some coffee. He turns and points down the hallway.

"Your sister and I used to sleep in that room at the end. She slept against the window, and I slept against the other wall, until we were about five, then we got sent to live with a family near billings. That family wouldn't let us sleep in the same room because they didn't like girls, so they kept us apart and put your sister in this other small room. She would sneak out at night and sit by my door, and we would hold hands through the bottom of the door and sleep that way. We were always so close. And it was hard, but we were together. We were running all our lives, it felt like. Did you ever feel that way?"

I told him yes, that it always felt like I was running toward something. I was running to him, and our sister, and our mother and father. There was a pull. This pull. A true ache. Of self. I couldn't find my way inside where I wanted to be, where he was.

"But now, brother, I am here with you, in the future."

eyes wide and a drive so fast

tasting air
dancing still
water wanna party with real indians
and splash the bank
and see the future
and take the dog it means
nothing to me.

shadow your best

Dreaming, I went for a walk with my sister down to the gas station, where I saw a CNN news reporter interviewing our brother on the corner about the new litter of puppies all born with a marking that looked like an american flag. I don't know why they decided to interview my brother in our town about the puppies because they weren't actually his puppies. And the puppies weren't actually from our town, but from the next one over, but I knew that when the news reporters came, they would scout the reservation for the person that looked the most Indian and the spot that looked the most like the wild west. A Warbonnet. A horse. By a river, or a mountain, or a cliff, or a butte, or maybe a mesa. But if you lived on a snowy, rural reservation, with one trade post, your interview would be on the saddest corner on the entire reservation.

This time, the interviewee was our brother, and the location was in front of the boarded-up car wash turned mechanic garage turned community shelter.

"This guy," my sister said.

We both walked up to him and crowded around the camera and watched my brother give this interview in real time, like he had been practicing.

He was hitting all the right notes: an introduction in Cheyenne, the importance of our ceremonies, and how sacred dogs are to our people. He said he was there when the puppies were born, and that it was he who had counted all fifty stars. He waved his hands with theatrical flair. They asked where he worked and he said he was a lawyer. The reporter seemed surprised until my brother added, "my own."

We laughed when my brother motioned to us.

Soon, the news reporter began asking us about the new puppies. My sister told the reporter that it was actually she who had seen the american flag first and she counted all thirteen stripes. She said she knew it was an american flag because she had seen one on tv before. She then said she knew there was something special about this litter because the mom was a wolfdog who became a ghost. My sister told this story:

> The dog froze to death and became a spirit. She would leave paw prints in the snow though she had no body and nobody saw her. Sometimes, when I would wake up and want to be warm again, I would see the spirit of this dog sitting beside the fire with one white bear. Sometimes they would stay, but other times they would go. I would listen to the spirit of this dog long into morning because she became a part of me. Like all the dog's ancestors before, I knew when the time came to tilt the earth, the dog would form thirteen parts of itself. And it would grow stronger. I knew the end would come and I would live to see her again.

The news reporter's eyes teared up.

My sister ended her story by saying how honored she was to receive the wolfdog's blessing to see the new earth under the midday sun and give testimony to the world under the american flag.

I chimed in, "But sister, you haven't told this story before. *What could it possibly mean?*" Meeting her eyes, I knew she was about to beat my ass. "And what do you know about america? You've never seen it before."

The CNN reporter decidedly ended the interview, shook our hands, and hopped into their van—just before my brother would ask them for a ride down the street.

the headlights shine toward you

One summer while I was visiting home, my brother, my sister and I turned on the history channel and watched a group of men scouring barns for old antiques across the country. My brother was sitting on the couch and my sister was eating a sandwich. Going to the kitchen, I overheard the men on tv talking about antique Indian motorcycles.

> *There's three Indians in the back of this truck, man.*

> *They're just laying here. I mean, this is the kind of stuff that dreams are made of,*

> *ya know, it keeps me up at night.*

> *What year are the Indians?*

> *The one on the right is a '46 Chief, I don't know if it's original paint, but it's never been a part of anything. It's barely been touched.*

Coming back into the room, my brother chuckled and said, "Shit, are they talking about us? Shit's probably worth more than all three of us combined. Have we ever been a part of anything?"

———

My brother, sister, and I never spent that much time together under the same roof of any building. We were always moving separately, but on the same plane. Apart but always affected by one another.

Being with them, I would overhear stories populated by the characters of their lives and pretend I knew who they were talking about.

"Is your friend, my friend?" my sister asks my brother. "Because he was sitting next to me at the bar and asked me to buy him a hot pocket so I gave him five bucks but he folded it and used it to pick the dirt from his fingernails and then got up to go outside and I never saw him buy the hot pocket."

My brother tells her yeah, he does that.

"So, I ordered a diet coke and really wished I had that five bucks because that was the last money I had and I wanted to spend it all playing mom's favorite song on the jukebox. Diet coke does that to me, it gets me feeling. It's probably the caffeine. I asked this white guy sitting next to me, if he could slice me in two and take me out in separate parts. He just looked at me. And then I said I was your older sister and he got up and walked away."

He was probably the owner, my brother says.

"And so, I kept ordering diet cokes because I'm not drinking right now and the bartender wouldn't take my money, which was good because I really didn't have any anyways. But I kept ordering them and watching the others play pool. It was the first of the month, so it was really busy and I overheard a story of someone getting dragged from a car when her jacket got caught in the door. And then I remembered it was me."

hover their grey

There is already snow on the ground and my mother is running up the hill. She is carrying a baby on her back. I meet her and she runs past me without saying a word. She is carrying a baby on her back, determined and fierce, and she is running past me. I watch her climb, grabbing the pine trees to make it all the way to the top. She drops the baby off at the top and my mother keeps running. I do not hear the baby, I cannot see the baby. But when I see a blanket, I ask my brother what is she doing? He tells me she went to the creek for water and came back with a baby. I let my thoughts go and watch the white blanket at the top, breezing in the wind.

The white people came and shuffled around the crowd of Indians at the bottom of the hill. And I stand there watching, but I still do not understand.

I see smoke coming from behind the mountain. The mountain is breaking and the smoke is

coming.

The baby is crying and my brother says

That is you.

closing my eyes to see straight

Looking at a black-and-white dog, I ask, "aren't we all dogs?" He looks back at me and says yes. Or, rather, I say yes, and he doesn't say anything at all.

Growing up without my brother and sister, I have been talking to dogs since I was quite young, and sometimes they talk back. I spent my younger days living alone, and being alone, waiting for a life eclipse. Waiting for a life eclipse. Waiting for a life eclipse. And even before it came, I always knew my life would be eclipsed and overwhelmed by someone other than me.

Throughout my younger entirety, I always felt like I had something to prove to others—about being, something that made it difficult to dance around the continental division of my existence. And when my mother gave me up to be a family, a thousand miles away from my home, alone and apart as an only child, in a place that felt anti-Indian because I was the only Indian, I'd ask—

mother,

   where did we all go?

tour of the hemispheres

I was nearly one when my mother gave me up. Being too young then, I couldn't question it and now as an adult, it's too late.

I knew she had to do it, so as not to give up on her and me both. That's why I had to leave, which is something I've tried reconciling with even if I always knew my fate, always knew I had two families and that the start of my life had two beginnings: one with my mother, and one with my new family. And it wasn't anyone's fault.

> *When you were in my belly, I'd talk to your mom and she'd make me laugh. Her texas accent. I'm surprised you don't have one. Some white people are good, and I knew your parents were good people because they kept you and raised you.*

Through what I didn't realize at the time was careful deliberation and care, my mother did not intrude while I was growing up—only calling me on holidays and birthdays. *I wasn't raising you, they were. You deserved a chance.* Strict with her boundaries and rules, she never told my father where I was, or even my siblings for fear that they'd tell him and he would find me. And later in their life, my sister said my mother stopped mentioning me at all. In passing, a relative would ask about me. *I guess she's doing okay.*

I didn't understand then, except circumstances are what they are. Life is a continuous again and again and again.

melting in whisper

Whatever the fates decided, my mother and I were doing the best we could. And not all truths are equal and it is difficult to know where to stop the division of a separation.

I love you little one.

mother,

    can things be different?

red is the only color i see

blood men can
do better if i can
be as Indian
as you let me be
if you let me braid
my hair it does not
mean i know how
to braid my hair

america takes
and peels away
all we know
we are

FELT FEELING ABUNDANCE in some other when

in the big open when

finding tomorrow

It has been said that Indians want to be left alone, but never actually be alone. Growing up and being the only Indian in your school, in your town, in the eastern half of your state, at a place where you open a history textbook and see pictures of "real" Indians doing "real" Indian things, like bathing in rivers next to a teepee, and your classmates ask you, "do you do that, too?" and I ask myself—*should I?*—and where your high school mascot is the Indians and that makes you feel like the only real Indian in the world, like the place you were from never existed.

But you know it exists because that is where your family lives—and every Christmas you talk to them on the phone and they tell you stories about home—and you ask

mother,

      where is the Indian in me?

running into and away

When my sister first began calling me, it was sporadic. Sometimes she'd call two or three times a month, sometimes from an unknown number. Sometimes, she would ask me how I was doing and how school was. I would always say good because it was. Nearly every time, I'd tell her the exact same thing I told her on the last phone call because she couldn't ever remember what we had talked about.

Despite her being out of it and having habits that were none of my business, I always looked forward to her calls, whenever they would come, because I would hear her voice, my sister's voice, the only Indian voice that I had heard all day, even all month. And sometimes, every now and then, when the sun shone through, clouds gone, she would tell me a story. A good story. A story about our brother. A story about our mother. A story about our mother telling a story about our brother. A story about our uncle. A story about her going up a mountain and falling down it. A story where she was both the winner and the loser. A story I always wished I was in.

And sometimes, she would tell me stories about our people and teach me how to speak our language, and sometimes, when I'd get bold and she'd get loose, I'd ask her if I could speak to our mother.

She'd always say no because she was out, and then quickly ask, "how are your parents?"

"Good, sister, they're always good."

there under an illuminated same

And when I didn't know the taste of bison, and fat, I was within the parameters of existing as I always don't—between the nix and sweet of tap water and river water; ice cubes and ice blocks—a place where the mountains are not mountains because to me they aren't called mountains but places where I've lived, sometime in my life—in the periphery of shapes and objects I once could have called home, placed there by the soles of the mother's hands and whatever water she drank from so that I could be inside—and then she told me the taste of her favorite fruit and I still don't know the taste of bison tongue but I can find the fat.

I do not see me.

Everywhere I see

—but not me.

october song

Over the next year, my sister and my brother began calling me more and more. My brother's voice, hushed like my sister's, would leave me suspended as he told me stories from his life, where every day seemed like a new day and time didn't exist. I'd never seen a street fight, or been in a police chase, or driven our cousins back from the hospital after a car crash. I never knew. During every call, he'd always ask me if I had grown any since the last time we spoke.

———

One evening, when I was fifteen, my brother handed the phone to my mother—and, for the first time, she wanted to know everything.

mother,

You heard me first

when I was a child I took my first steps to my grandfather in

my grandparents' kitchen and when my parents were working

downtown I had a nanny who kept me during the days and her

family was good to me and it was good for me because they

were brown too and in my mind I was a part of their family

and her kids were my sisters and brothers and it felt like home

again and when I was four I was in their daughter's

quinceañera and I looked like a flower girl and everyone spoke

Spanish to me and still does here and when I was a child I

understood but I don't now

when I was a baby I had a birthmark on my tailbone and the

doctor had to write a note to let the worried world know that it

wasn't bruises but a birthmark that Native children have it is

the mongolian birthmark and oh, you had one too then we

moved to the other big city but I grew up in the country where

I first cut my hair when I was seven and I keep it short and no

I've never braided it but it is too hot to have long hair in the

summer and there's a lot of mosquitos here I am a junior in

high school and class president and I got my learner's permit

and drive a truck yes I know how to swim

this last winter my family and I went skiing in wyoming oh

you know where that is you've been to those mountains

before and on weekends my dad and I go to Denny's when I

am not running cross-country last year I made it to state in
the junior olympics for running and got third place I didn't
know our family were runners and my cousin holds the
montana track record I am planning to go to college and run
track and maybe I'll make it I have a lot of friends and my
favorite color is red I eat a lot of okra and my favorite meal is
a chicken fried steak and it gets hot here I am about five feet
tall and do I look like you?
I didn't know wild sage grew in west texas what is sweetgrass I
don't go to powwows because there are no powwows where I
live I went to one once somewhere in oklahoma when I was
little there are no Indians in my town I haven't seen one since
I was little I am the only Indian in my school and it is lonely I
feel alone all the time being the only one and it's hard to be
this alone all the time when I don't look like anyone in my
family do I look like you
I want to know
you and hear your stories I am proud to be Cheyenne and I
know I come from a strong family but my family here is strong
too and I love my mom and dad more than anyone else in the
world and you too
are we more alike than different I can't remember

hymn eden

mother,

I am on my way to montana.

I am on the plane to come and see you. I am coming home this time because you told me it is time. I have just graduated high school and

I get off the plane and go down the stairs. I see my sister taking pictures of me.

She gives me the biggest, warmest hug that I could ever remember, and then I do remember.

I hug my brother, who says, well that was a long-short flight. I don't know if he means the flight I just took or the flight I took sixteen years ago.

Man, brother, you're so tall.

And you're so short.

We both laugh

and I see you crying.

It's so good to see you,

we told each other over and over.

how we're here

Huddled over beadwork, my mother handed me a folder filled with
pictures. I sat quietly beside her as I shuffled through a stack of photos
from when my siblings were in grade school. First grade, third grade,
sixth grade. Studying each picture, I'd see my nose on my brother's face.
My sister's eyes were my own. A younger picture of my mother would find
us holding ourselves in the same way. I glance at her in this quiet moment
and see her elbows resting softly against her body, her posture keeping her
limbs so close to her sides and her hands together, as she beaded, like she
was praying—and maybe she was.

My days spent at my mother's kitchen table or my dad's porch were never
enough. I sitting with my body folded with my hands together, sitting and
listening for hours. Hoping I could remember all of them. Even if I
couldn't, the full felt feeling remains.

you heard me first in the end

my red skin comes
from hot sun
you are my look in
the mirror the shine
forever i have seen
the finer things i have
seen the red door

red tilts home

After my father died, my mother and I would spend hours talking on the phone while I was in college. We became closer. She let me into her world, and it became ours. She told me enough to fill me forever. Stories about our history, our origins, our victories, where our names came from. Stories from her life, from her grandparents. And I'd listen and imagine where I fit into these stories. Of course, I was her daughter, but I also wasn't. Who is my mother if I already have a mom?

Is she a friend?

———

Looking at pictures of my siblings when they were younger, I wondered where I would have fit into my family. And if I ever would? Being the youngest, I was always looking up to them and watching them, in all the ways I could, being so far. Over the phone, in pictures sent through parcels, in the mirror—where even my voice wasn't my own, it was my sister's, too.

I didn't have the stories to tell me who I was growing up. I only knew how to be Indian through cartoons and tv, see what an Indian is and what an Indian does. Do I need an arrow and bow to feel better? And braided hair? I had the name and brow, but what made me feel real.

mother,

   how do you say I love you in Cheyenne?

I know Among twenty Indians I am one who has skin as coppery as a
penny and so does my mother I am not a half-breed but full and I am of
one mind and my heart is Red I tried riding a canoe but was told by a boy
scout it was a kayak and nearly fell in the water Horses don't scare me but
goats do My car has scars along its flanks from spatial misjudgments
when I pull into Sonic for a diet coke My kind of Indian has to be self-
defined It's whatever I do, however I do it.

Nemehoste.

Nemehoste is how you say I love you.

seeing the end

Determining whether my past is either incomplete or complete wrestles strong memories from wherever memory is kept Articulate (muddy) dreams and unfinished stories I heard from you and father keep me in motion I've tried to dart away but they attach themselves under different names wellness, religion, country I see america on tv and drive passing its flags to church They're big I don't have big enough words to reconcile what this image holds for the Indian me and I won't try It will take my life My own past is punctured holes of you Indian and family To try and become more than what I am in adulthood is a farce—when all america sees is an Indian with brown skin and black hair and therefore I am nameless And so I fill in the blank Me Growing and taking my parents' easy name as my own afforded me insulation from the judgments and rounds that would happen when my last name was overheard and I was too often asked if it was real And so I'd ask myself if I was real Shutting off memories is possible but to the detriment of self Healing is possible if you want it but it is never clear how Now you are now gone and so is father Brother and sister are here and I will never have the time to ask you why did it have to happen like this mother,

My mother is right beside me. She is holding my hand. She is walking beside me and together we go to my uncle's house to tell him that we had found the letter he was looking for. The letter that held all the answers together. A letter that appeared from the BIA, washington, d.c., office, ordering the sun not to shine on the reservation. My uncle opens the letter and gives it me. He is motionless and he is sad.

I tell him, *uncle, the moon will still shine.*

My uncle received the letter because he is the only elder that can see the future. The only elder that our people would listen to. The only elder that kept our stories. He could see

the white clay settling back into the earth and the grass returning aplenty before the whites came.

A 21st-century prophet. When he grabbed me by the shoulder, I shuddered,

Why the sun?

The moon kept itself high in the sky, and I kept the fire.

On the seventh day of darkness, I found my uncle, withered and small. He kept the flames alive with his stories. He knew the day would come when the u.s. government would take away the sun from the land because they had just about taken away everything else. He said he couldn't believe it.

As he spoke, a bird fell out of the sky. We grabbed the bird and threw it in the pot over the fire. It was a magpie, but we had to eat.

Feeling the warmth from the fire, and the light from the moon, I went down to the river to fish. I could tell they were biting. When I threw my line into the water, I felt the hook catch something heavy and reeled in my cast. From the water, I pulled out a red sweatshirt. It had our school's name on it. I squeezed it from the water.

When I got back to camp, I showed my mother the sweatshirt in the moonlight. She said it looked like the one my cousin would wear. Feeling the warmth from the sweatshirt, and the memory, I went down to the river and sat. I can't remember much about the last time I saw my cousin, but I remember it was Memorial Day weekend.

When my cousin went missing, I got questioned by my entire family for a long time. I sometimes still do. I don't remember a lot from that night, except that I was self-destructing, but in a healthy way. I don't smoke, I don't do drugs, I don't huff, I only drink. I was ripped up when my cousin wanted a ride back to town, but I lost her in the crowd. By the time I got back to my aunt's house, she wasn't there and when I woke up, she still wasn't there.

We searched every ravine and every path, from down in the valleys all the way up to the mountains. We searched the pines and we searched the creeks. By the time the searching was over, we found her shoes and we found her bracelet by the river. We never found her.

When the government ordered the sun to not shine on our reservation, I stayed close to my camp with my family and tended the fire. My mother stayed and my uncle prayed in the mountains. I couldn't remember when the nights came and went, but I do remember holding my mother's hand when she got hungry.

One night, I was lying down, sleeping, when my mother woke me up. She said she heard from the next town that Charla had come back. My mother grabbed me and told me to get up. We had to get up and go see her. So, I grabbed my bag and my knife and we headed out. Walking west towards town, I asked my mother who Charla was. She told me Charla was my dad's sister and one day she went to helena and didn't come back. She just disappeared. They always kept an eye out for her but had never heard from her. She never came home.

During our walk, my mother told me many Charla stories. Stories about dancing at powwows together, stories about going to new mexico to see her kids, stories about American Bar in gallup, or heading out to san francisco to Alcatraz. Stories about being sent to utah. My mother said I was too young to remember, but when I was a baby, Charla used to carry me around on her back in a cradleboard and walk the mountains. She couldn't believe they found Charla. How could Charla come back? Where was she, all this time? When we got to town, my mother started knocking on doors to see who had seen Charla. It was dark, and the moon was black.

Expecting the worst, my mother almost gave up, but the next door she knocked, opened. In the kitchen, my mother found a crowd gathered around Charla, who was sitting at the table. When Charla saw my mother, she got up and ran to hug her. I heard cries and laughs. My mother told her that she never thought she would ever see her again, but Charla said that she always knew she would.

Charla told us she never went missing. She was always there. She knew where she was at all times; she was the longevity of many parts, a place whereby Creator's technicolor united her with centuries of Tsistsistas who had peace within themselves and without. And she was happy. She journeyed through millennia. Indians loved more than others, she said, and while she could have come back home sooner, she didn't want to. When the Creator saw the sun darken, the Creator gave new light in the form of Charla's return.

Walking back to camp, my mother talked to me under the midday moon about how it was foretold darkness would overtake the land. She told me that when the land turns dark, the illumination of the moon will make the clouds turn white. The government would come to count and kill us before retaking our land and ordering the sun to shine again. We have survived a whole lot more than darkness on this land, she said, and it never lasts. She said this with such conviction that the bag on my back became lighter.

I pulled out my knife to kill a frog.

Though we had each other to lean on, months without the sun caused great confusion amongst our people. We grew smaller and into ourselves. Food started getting scarce and because the sun shined on the land on the other side of the reservation border, many of our people waited at the borderline for elk to cross. When our people left the reservation to go to billings, they never returned. There was only us.

One day—my birthday—as I was listening to my mother tell stories, I felt a tap on my shoulder. "Happy Birthday." Turning around, I saw my cousin. I hugged her and didn't let go.

"I knew you'd show up sometime," I said through tears.

"Where'd you get that sweatshirt?" she teased me, pulling at the red sweatshirt I was wearing. "I knew you stole it from my room."

I shook my head. "No, I found it by the river fishing."

"Man, I gotta learn how to swim next time."

We both laughed.

My cousin and Charla were not the only ones to return. Some were family members from many centuries ago that came to help and teach our ways of life. Some called them angels, some called them prophets, others called them ancestors. By the next winter, our people were the strongest I had ever seen. Our people had started praying again. By the time of the u.s. presidential election, the government reordered the sun not to shine, but the sun didn't listen.

will you look for me at all

mother,

I wasn't afraid to die, until you said you were. The way one feels
when someone's world closest to you crumbles and so yours does
too. The sight of seeing a marble Madonna crumble. Scared. Alone.
But you weren't catholic, you weren't mormon, you were spiritual
and a believer of God. god. The same god Cheyenne people believed
in, one single god, the Creator. Ma'heo'e.

Did you know I was raised baptist? And while I have thought
about renouncing all of their beliefs for the sake of resisting the
20th-century image of the good, obedient Indian, I fear death too
much. An Indian baptist. I am the pilgrim and the Indian at the
thanksgiving table and whose fault is that—but then who is to
find fault in anything. I was born and only from you.

And still, I feel my beliefs deceive me when I wonder whether an
Indian should hold the biblical sword that has taken so much from us. I
see our past hope wilt these fair cigarettes in my mouth, but to me, it's
all tobacco. I smoke tobacco when I think of you. Am I a future hope
disappearing? A manifestation of the baptist Indian's final form who
changed their name and cut their hair? I was born, but not just from
you—but from the spirit who rose from the dead. Do you see him?

Where are you?

My beliefs have kept me from this fear and yet

how must we be

party remember me
enough to split
your shadow

with my first
day of the week

i am Indian
because my mother
said so

tending inside
this counterfeit
nation

& steal the plans
of my youth

riding the highway 212

mother,

I am picking up speed and the ice is getting thicker. I am on my way to see you. I am coming to see you. I haven't been home in a couple years, but I am driving the miles back home.

The reservation always feels extraterrestrial, like the international space station—a condensed bubble of sky, clouds, sun and moon. Always surprised they are the same ones that rise above you. I look at the bare map on the bare road, which makes a two-dimensional map seem even flatter, and pass the familiar road signs.

I see the catholic church—the nicest building in town—and I see the river. I am looking at the river and remembering a story you told me about my sister.

You said she once got so drunk during a party, she fell into the river and forgot how to swim. Then, someone pulled her out. My brother says it was you, but you said it was him. My sister doesn't remember but she cried when she made it to land.

I also remember you telling me that the river was poisoned by the neighboring coal mines. You said that the fish in the river were sick and so was the river. I remember meeting a cousin for the first time one summer, when I visited home from college, who told me about the center of the universe. He was so happy to have finally met me because I was your daughter. He thought the world of you, so he thought the same of me. He called himself a river rat, and the next summer he drowned.

It is hard to think that a river who has fed and kept us alive has also taken so much from us. Poison in the shadow of coal mountains.

I pull into your yard and knock on the door. You answer and tell me to sit down.

You have been sick for a little bit of a long time and I know that. Now, your sickness is so loud it asks if I have ever thought of where I want to be buried.

I say, yes—wherever you are.

new mass

apart
does grass
flower

i never did it right
it being the emerging
rose wearing green

i see the world
around around around
me and she is

grey tinted on stacked
bodies and everywhere i
see there is a car going fast

———

a car drives around

me and we are close in air

if a mother I should be

come I find myself saying

daughter if I fall

let me

my god has many lovers

and when I got an envelope reading official u.s.
government mail from the department of interior I thought
my citizenship got revoked for being Indian but it was just
the government saying I now own .1478589 acres in
montana from my mother along with the .577363 acres I
have in oklahoma from my father

& the letter
says

> *I am the victor*
> *I wear the crown*
>
> *My god has many*
> *lovers who say this*
> *world is special*
> *and yours is not*

and the letterhead opens and eats itself telling me *jesus is the answer*
of peace.

Bodies buried in straight lines, inches from each other.

He says it's there. "There." He points toward another golfer, fifty yards away, who is putting near a cart.

"How do you know?" I think to ask, though I already know the answer. I am so far past myself and out of place, an Indian at a country club, that no map could help me find myself in the middle of a south dakota golf course.

————

On the north side of a cedar fence, I walk closer to a sign that reads:

ABSOLUTELY NO PLAY FROM CEMETERY.

I walk further into the cemetery and find a plaque on concrete.

NAMES OF INDIANS
BURIED IN HIAWATHA ASYLUM CEMETERY

LONG TIME OWL WOMAN 8–25–08

JUANITA CASILDO 6–22–08

MARY FAIRCHILD 4–29–07

LUCY REED 4–19–07

MINNIE LACOUNT 7–5–06

SYLVIA RIDLEY 6–12–05

EDITH STANDINGBEAR 5–13–05

CHUR-AH-TAH-E-KAH 1–2–05

OLLIE HOUSE 7–19–04

ASAL-TCHEE 2–11–09

ALICE SHORT 4–17–09

ENAS-PAH 9–30–09

BABY RUTH ENAS-PAH 10–14–09

AGNES SLOAN 2–14–10

E-WE-JAR 10–4–10

KAYGWAYDAHSEGAIK 10–14–10

CHEE 5–4–11

EMMA GREGORY 3–12–12

MAGWON 3–23–12

KAY-GE-GAY-AUSH-EAK 3–12–13

KAY-ZHE-AH-BOW 6–22–12

BLUE SKY 6–20–14

LOUISE MCINTOSH 4–12–15

JANE BURCH 2–1–16

DASUE 5–20–16

MAGGIE SNOW 7–10–16

LUPE MARIA 10–27–16

LIZZIE VIPONT 4–17–17

MARY PEIRRE 5–16–17

NANCY CHEWIE 2–7–18

RUTH CHIEF-ON-TOP 5–15–18

MARY G. BUCK 12–14–18

CECILE COMES-AT-NIGHT 8–12–19

MAUD MAGPIE 4–24–20

POKE-AH-DAH-AB 12–26–20

SITS-IN-IT 1–26–21

JOSEPHINE WELLS 6–29–21

A.B. BLAIR 8–6–21

JOSEPHINE PAJIHATAKANA

BABY CALDWELL 1–31–21

SALLIE SEABOLT 7–12–22

SELINA PILON 10–14–22

MRS. TWOTEETH 1–10–23

KAYZO (KAYSO) 3–27–23

JOSEPHINE DECOUTEAU 4–9–23

JESSIE HALLOCK 6–12–23

MARIE PANCHO 10–17–23

EBE SIROWBOY 8–11–28

KIGER 7–2–29

MARY BAH 8–25–30

CYNIA HOULE 1–19–32

DRAG TOES 2–24–32

CHARLIE BROWN

JACOB HAYES 10–4–27

TOBY 3–6–06

TRUCHA 11–17–05

HON-SAH-SAH-KAH 10–23–05

BIG DAY 7–3–05

FRED TAKSUP 2–6–05

PETER GREENWOOD 9–22–05

ROBERT BRINGS PLENTY 5–20–03

NADESOODA 2–8–08

TOISTOTO 5–17–08

JAMES CHIEF CROW 10–24–08

YELLS AT NIGHT 11–21–08

JOHN WOODRUFF 5–15–09

GEORGE BEAUTISTE 5–30–09

BAPTISTE GINGRAS 12–19–09

LOWE WAR 12–24–09

SILAS HAWK 5–12–10

RED CLOUD 12–7–10

HOWLING WOLF 3–30–11

ANTONE 4–4–12

ARCH WOLF 7–2–12

FRANK STARR 4–28–13

JOSEPH TAYLOR 9–20–13

AMOS BROWN 5–1–21

JAMES CROW LIGHTENING 3–8–21

JOHN MARTIN 4–4–22

RED CROW 4–8–22

JAMES BLACKEYE 5–6–22

ABRAHAM MEACHERN 11–10–22

ALOYSIOUS MOORE 5–12–23

TOM FLOODWOOD 9–29–23

JAMES BLACK BULL 2–9–26

BENITO JUAN 3–24–26

SEYMOUR WAUKETCH 6–1–26

ANSELMO LUCAS 12–19–26

CHICO FRANCISCO 4–21–27

ROY WOLFE 3–31–28

MATT SMITH 11–30–28

TWO TETH 7–18–30

PUGAY BEEL 9–14–31

HERBERT CONLEY 3–17–33

JACK ROOT 10–30–33

CHARLIE CLAFFLIN 3–2–14

JOHN HALL 5–27–14

AMOS DEERR 7–13–14

NE-BOW-O-SAH 12–18–14

THOMAS CHASING BEAR 2–2–15

DAN-ACH-ONGINIWA 3–29–16

JOSEPHINE BIGNANE 5–20–16

WALKKAS 1–21–17

STEVE SIMONS 10–8–17

JAMES TWO CROWS 11–26–17

F.C. EAGLE 9–5–18

ANDREW DANCER 11–21–18

APOLORIO MORANDA 1–14–19

HARRY MILLER 4–25–19

HERBERT IRON 5–20–19

FRED COLLINS 6–4–19

JOHN COAL OF FIRE 6–20–19

JOSEPH D. MARSHALL 11–21–19

WILLIE GEORGE 11–23–19

JAMES HATHORN 11–29–19

IRA GIRSTEAU 3–27–20

EDWARD HEDGES 5–21–20

OMUDIS 6–5–20

GUY CROW NECK 7–29–20

JOHN BIG 8–25–20

A. KENNEDY 2–19–21

I read your name.

grandmother—

mother,

    is this the end?

we slept at last

My mother named me right after I was born. I remember her looking so small and then so big. I was so happy. She was my lighthouse, and I was wrapped and warm.

I fell asleep and woke up a thousand years later and a thousand years before.

july 1969

he was on a flatline
to the sky beyond
the ocean near the stars

carrying future
from wooden ships
and grandfather's pleas
to never touch the stars

by those in this life
he believed

a walk on
the moon would help
him remember
laika & thank her

sacrifice he lit a cigarette
and burned cedar before boarding
the spacecraft and into the sky

on the moon he felt
human he was man
& could pray &
dance & speak

like a kennedy
the world would watch
him but he did not

care he could not
hunt these lands
had he found
ed the moon?

thee dog eyes
of america tell him
free, this land

through liberty's light
he raised
the AIM flag

thisiswhere

she exists
and she does not
exist in one
sum of

america,
you've taken
more than you've given

marble blood
—short doubt in a god chat

exodus

Peace and love be with you over this great land that rests between the two oceans, in all four corners and the four directions therein. It is with the light of the power within, that I speak on behalf of the Creator from above who sees and will be seen by those who free themselves from the victors that have plagued the earth below. It is I, who has been sent from the heavens above, who cast beyond the mountains that hold the blood of our people in the light between the midday suns. I stand here before you to tell you of the great mountain that will be shaken by those who live on the seven lands.

When I turn back and see the white skull of a buffalo that looks like me, I know that the tilt of its shadow will be cast on the land from the west that bears the most fruit. The white skull has four maple branches in its two eyes and a black cup in its mouth. The jawbone has been crushed by the weight of the black cup. The feet of the great beast have been taken in pairs and stretched into the ground below, the hooves plated in gold and the head covered in flax. Everyone who touched its broken jaw waited in line on the shores of the seven lands as they watched the great beast fall into the great mountain in the west. I fall at the feet of the buffalo and close my eyes. His face is shining like the sun.

Now, under the north star, I put my hands together and reach for the black cup in the remains of the buffalo's jaw but find Ma'heo'e's work incomplete. I fall below. I take my name to the hills and my eyes meet with the one who is in the sickbed. His name is lightning and thunder and I feel the beads of rain begin to hit my face before my voice cries out to the heavens above. I open my eyes and see a creature with only one eye and one wing emerging from the waves to take its place upright over the eastern sea facing west. I see the black cup in the creature's mouth. I hear an eagle. I fall down again.

I see the creature open the ocean and crawl back in through a door facing the east. I see honey drip from the creature's mouth and I smell the rain. The abyss will soon make war and the black cup will be filled with gold. I hear the cries of those on the seven lands below.

Then I see another creature, translucent, giving testimony to those below with a sword in its hand. It tells of those things which I do not say, and I count the words on its breath. I see one thousand magpies with one thousand black cups flying west and landing on the creature's back.

Those in the seven lands grab bowls to gather every raindrop before it falls on the land. Two buffalo calves appear and drink from every bowl before the magpies eat the calves.

Then those below tear the thousand black cups from the magpies' mouths and begin to drink the drops of rain they hold. The portion doubles, and all those on all the lands below have a drink.

The translucent creature collects the black cups and throws them into the sea for the creature within to devour.

Those who drink on the land that bears the most fruit have their black cups refilled.

The translucent creature pours his cup into the living waters of the earth below and into the rivers that empty into the sea. A single pearl forms in each of the lakes in the seven lands below and rests in the deepest part of the water, casting enough light to reign forever and ever.

Acknowledgments

Foremost, I dedicate this work and express my love to my mother and father who first loved me and to my mother and father who loved and raised me. I want to thank my brothers and my sister for their love—I will always love you more. I want to thank my grandparents for their unconditional love.

Importantly, I want to thank Ma'heo'e for his blessings and protection— for without him, I wouldn't know love.

I want to thank Sam Chang for her enduring support—this collection would not have been possible without her mentorship and care, truly. The time and attention she gave this collection remain immeasurable.

I want to thank the Iowa Writers' Workshop for giving me the opportunity to craft this work—and for the friendships I made. I want to thank my dear friends for believing in this collection and for consistently supporting me as I went along on this journey: Xochitl Gonzalez—I cannot thank you enough for your friendship and love—Marilyn Manolakas, Eliot Duncan, Red Danielson, Melvin Li, and Gwyneth Kelly. Furthermore, I wish to also thank Aimee Cryer and David McDevitt for their enduring friendship and love.

I want to thank my favorite poets who were my truest teachers at the Iowa Writers' Workshop—and who I consider some of my closest friends: Hajar Hussaini, John Bosworth, Abby Petersen, Marisa Tirado, Ruben Cota Jr., and Jon Stout.

I want to thank those who have been supporting me and my work since before I believed: Allyson Von Seggern, Jason Boyd, Kaitlyn Carr, and Kevin Hanlon.

I want to thank Claudia Ballard for her support and advocacy, and for believing in this work. It has been a wonderful journey to have you by my side. I also want to thank Allie Merola, who has given this collection incredible care and direction—and who I consider a friend.

I want to thank Dion Killsback for his continuous and generous support throughout the years.

I want to thank Gary Stuart for encouraging me to begin this journey and believing in me from the moment I submitted part of this work in his class all those years ago.

I want to thank Merlyn Redcherries—my uncle and fellow poet whose love for our Cheyenne people transcends me.

I want to thank my nation, the Cheyenne Nation, and my people for their love—and for the love of my ancestors who endured great sacrifice so that I could live.

I have always said my life wouldn't be so without love and prayer. To anyone who has ever loved and prayed for me from the earth to the stars, I thank you and I love you.

mother,

    this is for you.

A Note about "red tilts home"

The last section of this poem is written in response to Anita Endrezze's poem "Thirteen Ways of Looking at an Indian." Anita Endrezze is an author and artist of Yaqui descent. Her latest book of poems is "Enigma," published by Press 53.

M.S. REDCHERRIES received an MFA from the Iowa Writers' Workshop and a JD from Arizona State University College of Law. She is a citizen of the Northern Cheyenne Nation and lives in Brooklyn.